MEDIA IN ACTION

NEWSPAPERS

Susannah Foreman

Illustrated by Debbie Hinks

MEDIA IN ACTION

Newspapers
Advertising
Books
Television

HEINEMANN CHILDREN'S REFERENCE
a division of Heinemann Educational Books Ltd
Halley Court, Jordan Hill, Oxford OX2 8EJ

OXFORD LONDON EDINBURGH
MELBOURNE SYDNEY AUCKLAND
MADRID ATHENS BOLOGNA
SINGAPORE IBADAN NAIROBI HARARE
GABARONE KINGSTON PORTSMOUTH N.H. (USA)

First published 1990

Devised and produced by Touchstone Publishing Ltd
68 Florence Road, Brighton, East Sussex BN1 6DJ, England

British Library Cataloguing in Publication Data
Foreman, Susannah, *1957-*
Newspapers.
1. Newspapers
I. Title II. Hinks, Debbie III. Series
070.1'72

ISBN 0 431 00116 2

Typeset by JB Type, Hove, East Sussex, Great Britain.
Printed in Hong Kong

90 91 92 93 94 95 10 9 8 7 6 5 4 3 2 1

Contents

08·00 A Story!

Jenny is a reporter for the *Daily Messenger*, a national daily newspaper. She hasn't been in the job long and she is anxious to do well. Several of her stories have been printed in the paper but, like many reporters, she dreams of finding a story that will make front-page headlines. An early morning phone call from one of Jenny's contacts may give her the chance she has been waiting for.

A reporter must check all the details of a story before the paper will accept it. To be successful, Jenny must not give up. She will have to track down and interview Tony James' family to find out background news. She will have to talk to the rescue services handling the operation, and they may be very reluctant to talk to her. To get her story, Jenny must work long hours and travel long distances.

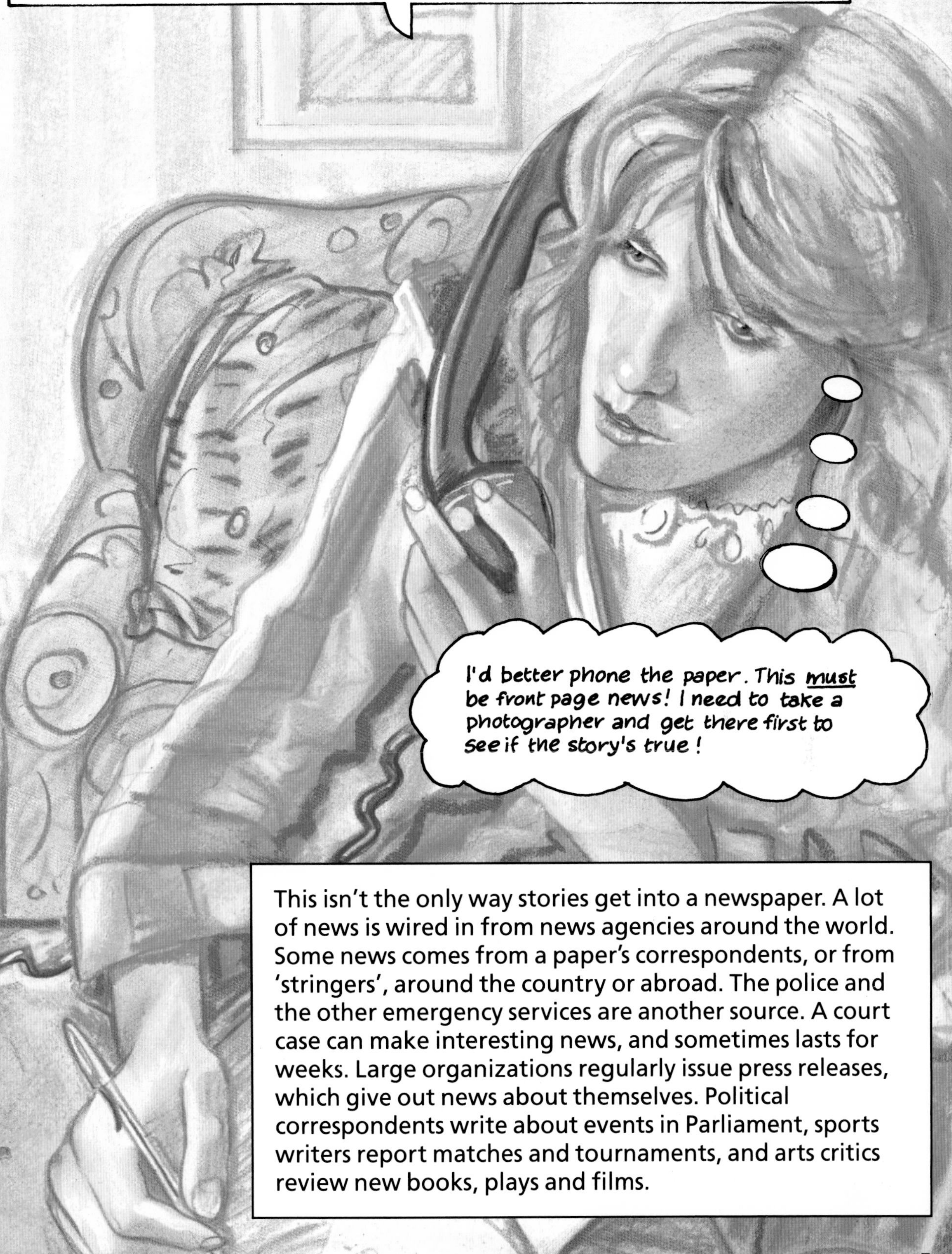

Can we go through that again? You say that Tony James the T V star and his young son are missing. Last seen yesterday afternoon when they set off to go rock climbing in the mountains. Bad weather set in last night. Right. Got it. Thanks for the information.........Bye.
I'd better phone the paper. This must be front page news! I need to take a photographer and get there first to see if the story's true!

This isn't the only way stories get into a newspaper. A lot of news is wired in from news agencies around the world. Some news comes from a paper's correspondents, or from 'stringers', around the country or abroad. The police and the other emergency services are another source. A court case can make interesting news, and sometimes lasts for weeks. Large organizations regularly issue press releases, which give out news about themselves. Political correspondents write about events in Parliament, sports writers report matches and tournaments, and arts critics review new books, plays and films.

11·00 News Meeting

Every morning, the editor of the *Daily Messenger* meets with the section editors, who are responsible for the different areas of the paper. They deal with foreign news, political news, special features, sports, and so on. They discuss the news of the day and follow up stories from the day before. Jenny has already phoned to tell the paper that a big story might be breaking and it has caused quite a stir. In the editor's office, the meeting is in progress.

This story of Jenny's should make the front page. But I'm not sure if it's headline news. What else do we have?

Reports are coming in of an earthquake in China. They're not sure of the casualty figures yet.

The editor is in charge of the paper and has the final say on what is printed. However, he relies on the section editors to give him up-to-date information. The political editor reports on Parliament, the news editor follows the major news stories of the day, and the features editor looks after non-news items, such as articles on fashion.

China's too far away. What about the motorway pile-up in last night's fog?
National newspapers cover national and international news and often provide detailed background information on events. Local papers, on the other hand, mainly report items of news that will interest people living in the region the paper covers, such as proposed motorway routes, or plans to knock down houses to make way for a supermarket. Many people buy both types of paper but they read them for different reasons. They might buy the local paper to look at the jobs pages or property classified columns, while they read the national paper for information on world issues.
That's the third this month. Motorway crashes aren't news any more – what about the Prime Minister's speech yesterday on unemployment?

11·30 Fashion News

The editor's meeting has given everyone a clearer idea of what will appear in tomorrow's edition of the *Daily Messenger*. The features editor has just finished an article on a new fashion designer. It has taken her several days of hard work to research and write. She's feeling pleased with it and is taking a photocopy of the article to give to the editor. The sports editor hasn't begun his piece yet, he's been waiting anxiously by the Fax for a message from abroad to arrive.

This fashion designer is all the rage. I hope the editor likes the article – he wants it in tomorrow's edition !

Looks great, Sylvia. 'Photos of the big match in Spain will be wired today. Report to follow.' Good. That's my main story.

Feature articles, such as items on fashion or travel, can be written well in advance. Very often, several feature writers will be at work preparing articles that can be fitted into any edition of the paper. These pages of the paper can be planned beforehand, while the news stories that come in during the day have to be fitted into the remaining space.

A Facsimile machine or 'Fax' enables printed messages or pictures to be transmitted via telephone lines all around the world.

12·30 On the Trail

After a long drive, Jenny and the photographer have arrived at the mountain rescue headquarters, where the rescue operation is being co-ordinated. Helicopters are scouring the mountainside but, so far, neither Tony James nor his son have been spotted. The news of his disappearance travelled fast, and the area is crowded with other journalists, TV crews and anxious fans. Jenny has managed to persuade Tony James' wife to talk to her.

Mrs James, when did you first decide to raise the alarm?
About 8 o'clock last night. They'd been out since 2 o'clock and a heavy fog had come down.
Luckily it wasn't too cold last night. So as long as they haven't fallen, we're pretty optimistic.
Many reporters dictate their stories over the phone to a 'copy taker' at the newspaper. Other reporters carry portable computers, which are connected to VDU screens at the newspaper offices. Photographers either develop their films and send in the photos via a portable picture transmitter, or they might rush the films back to the newspaper darkroom for processing.

13·30

Taking a Break

Back at the *Daily Messenger*, the pressure is on to get the rest of the paper ready on time. National and international 'hard' news stories are coming in to the newsroom continuously. The newsroom journalists must sift through all the reports and decide which, if any, may be important enough to go into the paper. However, the major portion of the paper is made up of 'soft' news, planned and written in advance. Two soft news journalists, the environment columnist and the agony aunt, are taking a moment's break when the motoring correspondent rushes by in a hurry.

I've just delivered my piece on water pollution. I think it's going to cause quite a fuss.

Weather reports, motoring news, problem pages, quizzes, competitions and special features are known as soft news. Soft news can be prepared a long time ahead, whereas hard news, which comes in to the newspaper during the day, has to be slotted into the paper at the last minute. Many of the journalists who produce the soft news are freelance — they work from home and send in their articles when they are ready.

15·00 The Pictures

Every newspaper uses photographs to add impact to its pages. Many of them are rushed to the paper by the news photographers, or come in daily from the press agencies. The *Daily Messenger* has its own stock of black and white photos, mainly of people and places, which it uses to illustrate some stories. The paper's picture editor is responsible, together with the editor, for the final choice of photos printed in the paper. The picture department is always busy and a motorbike messenger has just arrived with an urgent consignment of photographs.

Yes, the photos have just come in from the mountain rescue H Q. There's one of Tony James's wife. She's crying – it's a powerful image.

Most national newspapers publish cartoons to provide a daily, humorous comment on the news. Here, political cartoonist Steve Bell is at work on the cartoon strip he creates for *The Guardian* newspaper.

If the photo a paper requires is not in their own library, it can be hired from another picture library. There are specialist press photo agencies, that have hundreds of photos of current affairs and famous personalities. There are also general agencies, that can supply photos of just about anything to illustrate an article or background report. For technical information, maps or diagrams can be produced by the paper's design department.

16·00 Tele-sales

In the tele-sales department the phones have been ringing non-stop. Members of the public call in with their advertisements for cars for sale, properties to let, or articles for sale. The tele-sales staff type in the information on their VDU screens. The advertisements will not be printed in tomorrow's edition of the *Daily Messenger*, but are booked to appear in the classified section in a few days' time.

I'll repeat that. '1964 Austin Healey, British Racing Green, excellent condition, £15 000.' Can I have your credit card number please?
Yes, sir. It's 12 pence a word, minimum £5. But remember we have a very wide readership.

Newspapers frequently print 'advertorials'. These are special articles which attract certain advertisers. For example, a feature on holidays in France will have advertisements printed alongside it for travel agents, French villa companies, airlines and ferry companies, and even for local French restaurants and local specialist food and wine shops.

The advertising sales department of a newspaper is very important. Every newspaper relies on selling advertising space to earn money to fund the paper, whether it is a full-page advertisement for a large company, or the small ads in the classified columns. The newspaper's sales representatives try to sell advertising space to as many large companies as possible.

A missing cat? I think you'd be better off advertising in your local paper, or in a newsagent's window.
Yes, bold type certainly helps the ad to stand out.

17·00 Late Changes!

There are only a few hours now until the paper 'goes to bed' and the final version is sent to be printed. The editor has come in to the newsroom to talk to the news editor. The front page has been reserved for Jenny's story, but two important news stories have just come in – a large fire and a possible political scandal.

It's just been confirmed there's a large fire at a chemicals factory just outside the city. There's talk of evacuating the area.

Tom ! Sorry to interrupt ! News from our parliamentary source. A well-known M P has been accused of accepting bribes. He may have to resign.
Right. We'll hold the front page - there might be some changes. Tell the sub-editors.
The layout and content of a paper changes all through the day as stories come and go, or as more important ones take the place of less significant ones. Everyone working on the paper must be prepared to make changes late in the day. They must be able to work fast and with an eye on the clock all the time.

18·00 Page Make-up

Most of the paper is now ready, and the sub-editors have begun work on the skilled job of making up the pages. The subs are working quickly and accurately at their VDU screens, writing catchy headlines, editing and sometimes rewriting articles, making sure the columns of type fit the space allowed, and checking that photographs and diagrams are all in the right places. However, they are still waiting for the go-ahead to make up the front page.

O.K. I'll stand by for changes to the front page, but it's getting awfully late!
None of our journalists can spell!

This environment piece is too long. I'll have to cut it a lot to fit into two columns.

Before computer technology was introduced into the printing industry, newspaper type had to be set into position by hand. This typesetter is placing metal pieces of type in the right order to make up lines of text.

In the past, newspaper pages were made up by hand. Columns of type (galleys) and headlines were cut up and pasted down into position. Huge advances in computer technology mean that it is now possible to do all this on a VDU screen. At the touch of a button the sub-editor can change the layout of a page, move columns, reduce the size of the type, or enlarge spaces left for photographs, until the best page design is found. In the latest machines, the photographs (black and white, and colour) can even be included on the page.

20·00 Final Meeting

There's just over an hour until the deadline. The front page is always the last to be made up because it contains the most important news. The editor must decide now on the lead story so that the subs can lay out the front page before the printing presses roll. In the editor's office, a final meeting has been called. Jenny has phoned in from the mountain rescue HQ – and it looks as though her story is going to make the headlines.

The White House has just announced an international space programme to promote cooperation between nations. It should go in somewhere.
We can't go ahead with the bribery scandal. I can't get anyone to confirm it and we could be sued for libel.
The fire at the chemicals factory has been put out. But there's still a story there, and we've got some good pictures.
Newspapers must have proof of any gossip or scandal they want to print, or they could be sued for libel (that is, made to pay a great deal of money in 'damages' to the person concerned, the 'injured party'). The record amount for damages in the UK is £1 million, paid to singer Elton John by *The Sun* newspaper in January 1989.

22·00 Gone to Press

The *Daily Messenger* has 'gone to bed'. The paper is now being printed, so if any further news comes in it will have to wait for the next edition. The printers are now looking after the paper during the final stages. Throughout the night, the huge printing press will pour out over 200,000 copies of the newspaper per hour.

In the most modern processes, the made-up pages can be transmitted directly to the printers via the telephone line. This saves time and means that changes can be made at the very last minute. To speed up their delivery service, some newspapers transmit their copy to several different printers around the country. Communication satellites can send copy across the world for international editions.
For international editions of a newspaper, communications satellites can transmit made-up pages to printers across the world in minutes.
This isn't folding properly, it needs adjusting.

03·00 Loading Up

In the warehouse, automatically folded copies of the *Daily Messenger* arrive from the printers on a huge conveyor belt. Here, after being sorted into manageable bundles, they are loaded into delivery vans ready to be taken to the railway station, the airport and to many different places all over the country.

There you go, Jack. Your van's full. Where are you off to tonight?
I'm taking these to Manchester. I'd better get a move on.

la Repubblica
MAGLIA
MAGLIA
OGGI SI GIRA
LA STAMPA
TENNIS PER DIVERTIRSI
LA STAMPA
Foreign newspapers, from many different countries, can be bought from newstands in most of the world's capital cities.
Throughout the night, the *Daily Messenger* will be delivered to newsagents, ready to go on newstands up and down the country by the morning. Some copies will be delivered directly to people's homes, others to newstands in the streets or at railway stations, where commuters will buy their copies on the way to work. The international edition will be flown to most European cities
I'll just take these to the station, then I'll come back for the local delivery.
That lot's ready to go to the airport. Who's taking it?

08·00 The Readers

All yesterday's hard work has resulted in this morning's edition of the *Daily Messenger*. Although Jenny's story made the front page, it is no longer big news, because radio and television broadcasts reported it on last night's news programmes. The Johnson family have the *Daily Messenger* delivered every morning and they all enjoy reading it for different reasons.

I don't know why we buy a newspaper when you can hear all the news on the telly.
We're now going over to an interview with Tony James and his son, who spent a comfortable night in hospital following last night's dramatic mountain rescue.

In the past, people waited eagerly for the newspapers as they were the only source of news. But with the advent of radio and television, both of which announce the news as it happens, newspapers have lost this function. We buy newspapers for many reasons. They are portable and can be dipped into whenever we have a moment, they give far more information than a TV news programme can on a particular issue, they have crossword puzzles and weather forecasts, and a daily editorial comment. It is because they have so much to offer to so many different people, that they will continue for many years to come.
Can I have the TV page, Dad? I want to see if there's a good film on tonight.
You only get the headlines on the TV. I like to read about the news in detail.
Hurry up with the paper, Dad. I want to read about that new fashion designer.

Glossary

Advertorial An article printed together with certain advertisements.

Breaking A story that is breaking is new and unexpected and still running its course.

Classified ads The small ads in newspapers, usually placed by members of the public.

Communications satellite A satellite used to send radio, television and telephone signals around the world.

Copytaker A person who types out a news story as it is dictated over the phone.

Correspondent A journalist with a specialist subject, eg a political correspondent.

Damages Money paid to the injured party in a libel case.

Deadline The time an article or a newspaper must be ready for printing.

Edit To correct, sometimes rewrite stories, and make them fit the allowed space.

Edition A published newspaper.

Features Non-news items, such as articles on fashion or travel.

Foreign correspondent A journalist who works for a newspaper but is based abroad.

Freelance To be self-employed.

Galleys Printed columns of type.

Hard news The latest news, which is reported immediately.

Layout The position of the words and pictures on a page.

Libel A written, published statement which is said to damage a person's reputation.

News agencies Organizations around the world who collect and report news, which they pass on to newspapers for a fee. Also called press agencies.

Newsroom The place where the hard news journalists work and where the latest news and stories arrive.

Page make-up Laying out the newspaper pages on a VDU screen, ready for printing.

Picture transmitter A small machine used by photographers, that can 'wire', or send photographs down a telephone line, back to the newspaper.

Scoop A news story reported in one newspaper, ahead of the others.

Section editors The people in charge of the different subject areas in a newspaper, eg. the foreign news editor.

Soft news The articles in a newspaper that are prepared in advance, also 'non-news' items like crosswords and readers' letters.

Stringer A freelance journalist, often based abroad, who works for several papers.

Type Lettering.

VDU Visual Display Unit. A computer, made up of a screen, keyboard and a memory, which is used for storing information, editing and page make-up.

Wired Stories and photographs sent via telephone lines, often from abroad.

Useful addresses

Newspaper Publishers' Association
6 Bouverie Street
London EC4Y 8AY

Newspaper Society
Whitefriars House
6 Carmelite Street
London EC4 2BY

National Council for the Training of Journalists
Carlton House
Hemnall Street
Epping
Essex CM16 4NL

Picture Acknowledgements

The publishers would like to thank the following for the photographs reproduced in this book:

Cover, ZEFA Picture Library; p.9 Topham Picture Library; p.14 Paul Scheult/Eye Ubiquitous; p.21 ZEFA Picture Library; p.25 ZEFA Picture Library; p.27 Topham Picture Library.

Index